Demos is an independent think tank committed to radical thinking on the long-term problems facing the UK and other advanced
industrial societies.

It aims to develop ideas – both theoretical and practical – to help
shape the politics of the twenty first century, and to improve the
breadth and quality of political debate.

Demos publishes books and a regular journal and undertakes
substantial empirical and policy oriented research projects.
Demos is a registered charity.

In all its work Demos brings together people from a wide range
of backgrounds in business, academia, government, the voluntary
sector and the media to share and cross-fertilise ideas and experiences.

For further information and
subscription details please contact:
Demos
Panton House
25 Haymarket
London SW1Y 4EN
Telephone: 020 7420 5252
Facsimile: 020 7420 5302
email: mail@demos.co.uk

Other publications available from Demos:

After Social Democracy:
Politics, capitalism and the common life
John Gray

Civic Entrepreneurship
Charles Leadbeater and Sue Goss

The Creative Age
Kimberly Seltzer and Tom Bentley

The Employee Mutual:
Combining flexibility with security in the new world of work
Charles Leadbeater and Stephen Martin

The Rise of the Social Entrepreneur
Charles Leadbeater

For further publications information
please contact Demos.

Entrepreneurship and the wired life

Work in the wake of careers

Fernando Flores and John Gray

First published in 2000 by
Demos
Panton House
25 Haymarket
London SW1Y 4EN
Telephone: 020 7420 5252
Facsimile: 020 7420 5302
email: mail@demos.co.uk

ISBN 1 84180 020 1
Printed in Great Britain by Redwood Books

Contents

Acknowledgements   **7**

The last days of the career?   **9**

New forms of working life: the wired and the entrepreneurial   **21**

Policy in the wake of careers   **35**

Notes   **47**

About the authors

At 29, Fernando Flores was Minister of Finance in Chile, in the government of Salvador Allende. After some years of imprisonment by the Pinochet regime, he moved to California, where he established his innovative business management consultancy company, Business Design Associates. His most recent book is *Disclosing New Worlds* (MIT Press).

John Gary is Professor of European Thought at the LSE. His most recent book is *False Dawn: The delusions of global capitalism* (Granta).

Acknowledgements

We wish to thank Werner Ahlers who worked resourcefully and tirelessly as our researcher on this project. For their valuable comments we are indebted to Tom Bentley, Ian Christie, Charles Leadbeater, Geoff Mulgan, Richard Sennett and Charles Spinosa. All the usual disclaimers apply.

The last days of the career?

The career, as an institution, is in unavoidable decline. The emergence of knowledge-based economies means the creative destruction of many time-honoured practices, including those at the core of traditional career structures. This change implies a fundamental shift in the attainable aspirations of the working majority, but so far it is little understood. Public policy is still based on promises which assume careers to be the model for desirable employment. As a result, government investment in workforce education is too narrowly focused on reskilling for new careers – a shallow response to the pace, scale and depth of change we face. It is not just that most people must expect more jobs in a lifetime, or to have to switch vocation. The very idea of a career now makes less and less sense of most people's working lives.

Many of the practices and institutions we inherited from earlier phases of the Industrial Revolution are ill-suited to the world of work which is now taking shape. A new, entrepreneurial approach to preparing for working life is needed, together with reforms of productivity's infrastructure – pensions, taxation, credit and the like – and a basic alteration in education. In this pamphlet we seek to establish a foundation for such reforms in three ways. First, we examine the ongoing dissolution of the career as the preeminent model of working life, to which most have aspired and which many have achieved. Second, we examine the new forms of working life emerging in its wake and their implications for individuals and communities. Finally, we consider how public policy can best respond to these changes.

Why careers matter

In its original English uses, 'career' meant a path or road, and its later meaning is an extension of that usage. A career was a lifelong pathway through the world of work, a single vocation or calling that individuals adopted in early maturity that they often prepared for from childhood. Careers were pursued throughout the whole of individuals' working lives. In the latter half of the twentieth century, careers provided steady job tenure in an established professional culture and, for many, progression within an organisational hierarchy.

The corrosion of this institution is the principal economic challenge facing the working majority in late modern societies. Centre-left parties and governments, who see their role as extending the advantages and opportunities of middle-class life to all, have poorly understood the causes and consequences of its decline. With the obsolescence of the career, one of the central planks of middle-class life is removed.

The career has been a core social institution of twentieth century industrial civilisation. Though most may never have had full access to it, a career has been the most important route to achieving the personal autonomy to which most still aspire. Through careers, people could establish continuity and meaning by being the authors of their economic lives. Whether in law, medicine, manufacturing, government or any number of other domains, one's career could advance with increases in specialised knowledge and skill. The career has also played a crucial role in strengthening communities, by conferring a high value on local knowledge and relationships. As such, the career has been one of the central institutions legitimating dynamic market economies. As the basis of market economies shifts, the decline of the career risks depleting that legitimacy throughout society, particularly in the middle classes where care for the career has been strongest.

There are two primary moral hazards attached to the decline of the career. First, by undermining people's ability to choose stable and meaningful employment, it endangers the liberal values that modern market economies are meant to embody. Simultaneously, along with increases in labour mobility and the corrosion of many traditional values, the decline weakens the ties of local social cohesion on which such economies depend. Over time, these moral hazards could represent political risks for parties of the centre-left, which have in recent times attracted increased middle-class support. Even in the absence of a major economic setback, disillusioned middle classes are fertile grounds for a comeback of the right.

The fact that a traditional career is no longer a reasonable aspiration for the working majority creates both perils and opportunities that no advanced capitalist society has yet grasped. There have been signs that many countries are beginning to appreciate the importance of such changes, for example the workforce casualisation of the Clinton administration and the UK's lifelong learning.[1] These programmes, however, are usually attempts to assist citizens in realising career *changes*. They are not adequate responses to a world where growing numbers of people are continuously required to redefine their roles in society.

The corrosion of careers has largely been experienced as a diminution of control over one's life. This loss of autonomy is experienced most palpably by people whose career paths have been abruptly terminated by downsizing. It remains a pervasive fear for those whose current prospects have increasingly been called into question. The issue people face today is not merely job insecurity, but more the loss of meaning that occurs when working life no longer has a discernible shape.

Richard Sennett has documented this instability in his recent book, *The Corrosion of Character*.[2] As Sennett has shown, even those who successfully navigate the new uncertainties, moving from project to project can find that they are anxious about raising their families. They cannot find in their work lives any values to underpin the forms of continuity that are important for raising children, family warmth and neighbourly trust. They awkwardly announce themselves as followers of 'traditional' values while adopting lives which disconnect them from sustained productivity, neighbourhood and intimacy.

Sennett hopes that traditional social democratic policies can revive the forms of continuity which governed work and neighbourly life in the past. But the forces bringing about the decline of the career cannot be arrested by the policies of the past. Nor are sterile neo-liberal nostrums about labour flexibility and market efficiency useful responses to the new world of work. New thinking about individuals' economic lives is needed. This thinking must be ready to accept the demise of the career and take it as an opportunity to foster new working practices. The economic environment that sustained the institution of the career cannot be retrieved. The challenge is to understand how working life can, alongside economic productivity, again be made to serve both personal autonomy and social cohesion.

Why careers are in decline

While the causes of the career's decline are many, three are particularly significant: new technologies, the increasing customisation of products and services and the impact of globalisation on local knowledge.

New technologies

New information and communication technologies are spurring the dissolution of many industries and occupations. Service industries that mediate between buyers and sellers are particularly vulnerable to technological displacement. Travel agents, sales people in retail stores and much of the banking sector will survive only in leaner, more specialist forms. As early as 1993, Bank of America circulated an internal memorandum estimating that 'soon, only 19 per cent of the bank's employees will work full-time'. Non-bank banks such as Charles Schwab in the United States are offering investment and saving facilities along with chequing and lending programmes. Others are going further by offering these services over the telephone or online only.

Consumer banking is not alone in this displacement. Many careers will no longer be viable because the industries in which they were embedded will have disappeared or altered radically. The worldwide web's effect on the publishing industry, for example, is likely to be enormous. With technologies for book production and distribution made available to anyone through the web, the one value-added task left over from the current publishing industry will be the editorial function of determining what is worth reading by whom. Even this supposition assumes that the new technology will not displace the finished book. We could easily find ourselves with a revival of early-modern practice where manuscripts circulate, receive additions by their readers and do so without ever having a prepublication editorial review.

Another effect of new technologies has been to expedite the restructuring of firms. The re-engineering of business corporations has removed entire echelons of employees. Much of this re-engineering has had mixed results because the new technology that motivated and organised the restructuring was itself misunderstood as information processing equipment. In fact, the new technologies do something far more radical: they enable a more effective and sensitive coordination of economic life, achieved at much lower cost. As these new technologies are understood as coordination tools, additional displacements will occur with much better results for customers and shareholders. For employees, however, they will mean the disappearance of many more layers of activity.

As a result of the current restructuring, many expectations of traditional promotion have ceased to be realistic. As this happens, it becomes harder to recruit and retain people into large, hierarchical organisations. Bright people prefer to go into smaller business start-ups, where they can establish both their own ideas and their fortunes. During the 1990s, new incorporations in the US, already the highest in the industrialised world, grew by over 20 per cent in just five years.[3] In the UK, the number of enterprises grew by over 50 per cent between 1980 and 1996.[4] These start-ups are the winds of Schumpeter's gale of creative destruction, blowing through large organisations and stimulating mergers, restructuring, bankruptcy and rebirth on a large scale. As companies have become more fungible, they have ended many forms of stable, traditional employment within them.

Employment growth statistics give evidence of this trend. In the US between 1992 and 1996, companies with fewer than twenty employees grew on average by 13 per cent, those with between twenty and 100 grew by 4.5 per cent, and those with between 100 and 5,000 by only 1.8 per cent. Larger companies contracted by 1.7 per cent.[5] These numbers do not include independent contractors whose numbers rose by 70 per cent in the US during the same period.[6] Nor have these changes been restricted to the US: self-employment created three out of four new jobs in Canada between 1991 and 1995,[7] and self-employment in Britain has grown from 8 per cent to 15 per cent of the workforce in under twenty years.[8] In addition, over two-thirds of Britain's enterprises have no employees and, as of 1994, only 11 per cent had more than five.[9] While it is tempting to dismiss such trends as cyclical adjustments, many of these numbers do not encompass the recent recession, or reflect the downsizing and restructuring of the 1980s.

In another important trend, companies are now replacing traditional employees with cost-effective and flexible contractors offering 'business services', the fastest growing industry in both the US and UK. In Britain, large firms in business services such as management consultancy saw 20 to 30 per cent annual growth rates in both employment and employee turnover throughout the 1980s.[10] In the US between 1982 and 1992, overall employment rose by 22.7 per cent compared to 60.5 per cent in the business services industry. The largest employer in the United States, with more than double the workforce of General Motors, is Manpower, which provides temporary employees to organisations of all sizes. Such 'employee leasing' companies in the US grew from 98 in 1984 to well over 1,300 in 1993,[11] and they now employ more than three times as many people as they did in the early 1980s.[12]

The *breadth* of this trend is impressive. Of the 75 per cent of US companies hiring these 'contingent workers', more than half use them to acquire 'specific expertise',[13] contradicting the perception that 'temps' are restricted to non-professional roles.[14] In fact, numbers of *temporary professionals* in the US are growing twice as fast as other temps, and agencies providing them tripled in number between 1990 and 1994.[15] Correspondingly, over 55 per cent of all independent contractors are now categorised as managerial, professional speciality or sales,[16] a number which has climbed steadily since the 1980s.[17] By many estimates, 30 per cent of the US workforce is 'contingent'.[18] In Britain, the numbers of self-employed business people rose over 50 per cent during the 1980s and early 1990s.[19] The *Oxford Review of Economic Policy* estimates that the number full-time workers on indefinite contracts (that is, workers with careers or jobs modeled after careers) in Britain comprised only 50 per cent of the workforce in 1995 and was estimated to fall well below 40 per cent by 2000.[20] Already, almost a quarter of Britain's workforce is part time – higher than the US or any western European nation.[21]

Customisation and customer sensitivity

A second driving force is the growing focus on customisation of products and services. A new concern for customer convenience and lifestyle has led to a shift away from the production and distribution systems geared towards standard needs. This shift has thrown businesses into flux as they compete on unfamiliar ground. Strategists carefully analyse which corporate competencies produce the most value for customers, leading companies to re-organise and outsource many areas of their work. Outsourcing has turned more of the workforce into journeymen and women who market and sell their skills to many buyers. The quality movement, just-in-time delivery and the new customer orientation have also caused many managers to reconceive themselves as internal customers. This trend has transformed old careerist salary structures into more entrepreneurial pay-for-performance programmes. As each segment of an organisation reconceives itself as a business in its own right, compensation becomes more variable. On Wall Street, for example, typical performance pay ranges from 100 per cent to 200 per cent of nominal pay. In Britain, the Inland Revenue estimates that over 20 per cent of all rewards are comprised of merit pay structures.[22]

These responses to customer sensitivity and technological innovation are ongoing. The new economy is defined by perpetual change, and the responses of governments and people – even those intended to moderate the speed of change in the new economy – will bring about further transformations in productive life. The advantages of customer sensitivity for product innovation, customer retention and achieving the cost advantages of information technology will force innovation into fields where professional power is still strongly entrenched. Even traditional careers such as medicine and law are not immune from these pressures for change. For instance, in the United States, the growing diversity of health care techniques and willingness of insurance companies to pay for them is already leading to new managerial and cross-over professional roles, selling a wide array of health care services according to demand.

Today, when we are concerned about our health, we not only see our general practitioner, but also physical therapists, trainers and chiropractors, not to mention a whole host of alternative practitioners. The continuing focus on the patient will make traditional distinctions between these occupations more permeable. In the world of work we are entering, the lifetime of useful professional knowledge and occupational categorisations will be brief.

Globalisation and local knowledge
The third change has even larger implications. Globalisation of new technologies is making redundant many kinds of local and specialised skills that informed careers in the past. By globalisation we do *not* mean

the regime for world trade, capital flows and the increasingly homogenous markets that has prevailed over the past decade or so. We mean the worldwide diffusion of new technologies, which will go on regardless of the current regime's future.[23] We are not suggesting that this diffusion of new technologies makes *all* old skills redundant. New technologies, by themselves, cannot do many things. They cannot supplant friendship or family life, eliminate the long haul of politics or do away with the constraints of time and mortality that are common to us all. They *are*, however, transforming the contexts in which we work, partly by making many traditional sorts of local knowledge less useful.

Many careers developed around apprenticeship practices, in which practical knowledge accumulated over a working lifetime and was transmitted between generations. Such knowledge was embedded in local networks, communities and practices. But the effect of information technologies is often to scatter local working communities. Industrial clustering notwithstanding, the networks on which businesses rely are increasingly remote; dealers and suppliers are not only many thousands of miles away, but may belong to different business cultures. New kinds of local knowledge do come into existence. For example, in Silicon Valley, aspiring software entrepreneurs seek local knowledge of the venture capitalists who work in offices along Palo Alto's famed Sand Hill Road. They want to know how to get meetings with them, or which ones will be most sympathetic to a certain project. But venture capitalists are spreading and changing. In any one cluster of industries, the value of both geographically and professionally based local knowledge decreases.

In this new environment, relationships of trust are built out of increased transparency in costs, frankness about interests, assessment of performance, and recognising and respecting unfamiliar identities. Familiarity is no longer the basis of trust. Local networks are less and less the ground of a career. Local knowledge has a shorter shelf life. As industries change rapidly, skill in coping with new social contexts is often more useful than slowly built-up understandings of established social milieux. Older workers risk becoming useless repositories of obsolete local knowledge. Perhaps more than any other factor, the increasing obsolescence of local knowledge explains why the career's decline is irreversible. When businesses and industries are metamorphosing constantly, this type of knowledge loses its bearings. The world that forged it and made it useful is lost.

These three forces – technology, customisation and globalisation – are integral to the creativity and productivity of dynamic market economies. We all understand that the future belongs to knowledge-based economies. Yet we have not fully grasped the fact that careers, and the ways of acquiring and using knowledge that they embodied, are decreasingly productive in these economies.

To be sure, the career is not declining at the same rate in every domain, nor are its consequences the same in different economic cultures. Some professionals, such as judges and academics, have remained insulated from the forces rendering careers obsolete. Some workers – unskilled labourers and some categories of office workers, for example – have never had careers. Some so-called careers – in sports, fashion and parts of the arts and entertainment industries – have always been shorter than the normal working lifetime. In addition, entrepreneurial business activity has always had a different rhythm from that of the career. We shall see below how entrepreneurs' working lives have something of relevance to teach us about work in the new economy along its different courses of development

The new economy
At this point it is worth emphasising how pervasive these changes are. We have only seen the first wave of the new economy. Global markets, for instance, so far only exist for physical commodities like petroleum and timber, manufactured commodities like gasoline and aluminum, scale-driven businesses like aircraft engines and semiconductors, productivity-driven consumer goods like cameras and automobiles, and certain kinds of finance. Other goods and services are sold in national and local markets. Though we believe that local differences will matter more than most now think, even local economic regions will, in their own ways, be transformed by the underlying drivers of change.[24]

Though most evident in Anglo-Saxon free-market economies, these changes also affect social market economies in continental Europe and Asia. At least in part, higher rates of long-term unemployment in continental Europe are responses to the changes which in Anglo-Saxon countries have casualised significant sections of the work force.

Precisely how far unemployment in continental Europe is driven by these trends is disputed, but the policy differences are, in the long run, irrelevant. Neither structural labour market reform nor Keynesian reflation can be more than stop-gap policies, just as retraining for new careers is a shallow response. Across the whole of Europe, the emerging economic circumstances will require a new approach.

Ethics and the decline of careers

To a considerable extent, the social division of labour into discrete professions and careers is obsolete. Knowledge-based economies will rely less on static, industry-specific occupations and more on the continual restructuring of information and technology to meet fluctuating demand. While this restructuring addresses our preferences as consumers and as producers, the human needs that our careers have served are not withering away. No patterns of working life that fail to meet them will be humanly durable or politically legitimate.

Careers did several things for those who had them. A career bound together the phases of the working life, enabling people to shape a coherent narrative from it. At the end of their working days, people could view their careers as defined by the continuity of a lifetime's vigorous activity, rather than a string of disjointed experiences and additions to a 'portfolio'. Furthermore, when the career was connected with ideas of vocation or calling, it conferred meaning on life by nurturing the sense that each individual had a particular mission. Careers disclosed a world of meanings within which highly individualised choices and even random events became intelligible. This tells us something important about work, identity and personal fulfillment. That is why careers were the ideal of working life.

Most people have never understood their working lives in terms of self-invention or existential choice. Historically, they have assumed that in choosing work, each of us has to maintain an attuned ear to make a once-in-a-lifetime choice when a calling is discovered. In modern times, the career was a vehicle for this idea. A career shaped individual aspiration by promoting projects of long duration. It encouraged people to live their lives as exercises in productive engagement, rather than as successive episodes in want-satisfaction. People with careers did not experience themselves solely as economic resources; they derived fulfilment from a career as a vehicle for productive agency. The career opened up a world in which necessary adjustments to market forces were experienced as expressions of autonomous agency rather than passive adaptation or alienated submission.

In these respects, the role of careers in working life resembled that which Kant and Hegel claimed private property played. Like property, a career permitted human subjects to inscribe personal signatures on their lives. By working on themselves to attain the skills worthy of a profession, people were able to recognise their own identity and have this identity recognised by their communities. The career has played a crucial, if not the primary, role in giving people their personal identities in modern industrialised societies. We still identify people by their careers. With the decline in careers we begin to lose the sense of identity, autonomy and connection to others that they have provided.

The founders of European social thought recognised the social and psychological benefits of dividing labour into well-defined professions and occupations. Emile Durkheim saw it as a remedy to anomie—the malady of infinite aspiration which he thought individualist cultures were especially vulnerable to. For Durkheim the career was a valuable, perhaps even indispensable, modern institution. By contrast, Marx saw the division of labour into discrete professions and careers as a threat to personal autonomy and social solidarity. He feared that the growing division of labour in society would increase the alienation of workers from their labour and each other.

Marx's fears were not without precedent. Adam Smith anticipated them in *The Wealth of Nations*. Smith feared that the 'detail worker' of early industrialism would be lacking in education, civic spirit and the martial virtues. In *The German Ideology*, Marx articulated a utopian vision in which the social division of labour had largely withered away, partially as a response to fears he shared with Adam Smith. With the end of the career, we can see how much more prescient Durkheim's vision turned out to be. The fears that pervade working life today concentrate on the social marginality that follows long-term exclusion from employment and, more profoundly, the dissipation of meaning that comes when work has been deeply casualised. Consequently, Marx's fears of a society that lacks cohesion because it suffers from an economic system whose members are imprisoned in a minute niche in the division of labour have proven largely unfounded.

When working life was organised by careers, work disclosed a world that bore a personal signature, written in a text of professional expertise and enhanced by the tacit local knowledge that animates particular vocations. In the past, centre-left parties could reasonably promise that ever-expanding groups of people could enjoy the economic, social and personal goods of career-like work. Today, however, our personal signatures must be written in a different text, one given by a continual refinement of our basic skills as social beings. The world of meaningful work previously disclosed by careers must be replaced by the models of productive life being created by the forces described earlier.

The decline of careers signifies a loss of three key ethical goods. First, careers are the means by which most people directly participating in labour force focus their identities. They make a lifelong commitment to be a manager, engineer, lawyer, physician or the like. Such a commitment enables them to make plans about their training, income, lifestyle and family development. Moreover, with a career, that commitment becomes public and can be evaluated by those in the same vocational community. A career brings the recognition of that community to its bearer.

Second, careers provide a place in a broader civic community. A financial officer in a company could be seen as a candidate for church or local municipal treasurer. Likewise, a doctor or a pastor might be sought as a volunteer for many public organisations such as local fire departments or sports associations. Careers enable people to play roles as responsible citizens and, in return, playing these roles enhances their careers.

Third, careers give people a sense of autonomy, of being authors of their own lives. Careers do this by being embraced as a person's own vocation and in providing people with the wealth, time and self-respect to engage in activities that define the kind of people they take themselves to be. Thus, careers enable people to engage in lives of experimentation that change and enrich their self-understanding. Even more important, people with careers sense that they are the authors of their own lives by becoming more expert at the skills required of the career. How do people make sense of their working lives when careers are no longer available to them?

New forms of working life: the wired and the entrepreneurial

As careers die, two significantly different forms of working life are emerging in Western societies. On one hand, there is what we will call a 'wired' (fast, globally networked, project-centred) form of productivity which is emerging in Silicon Valley and other high-tech and media centres. Wired productivity creates new social goods and ethical values which replace and diminish our esteem for the traditional careerist values. On the other hand, a form of working life is emerging which accentuates other new values, but can support the traditional social goods of the career in new ways. We call this entrepreneurship, keeping in mind its social, political and economic forms. In practice, many working lives are both wired and entrepreneurial. Understanding these emerging ideals will enable us to form social policies that successfully address the death of careers.

Both the wired and entrepreneurial lives have their roots in well-known ideals from the past. In *The Genealogy of Morals* and other writings, Nietzsche's description and idealisation of the life projects of noblemen in the ancient and early-modern worlds closely approximates our account of wired life. This is a life animated by virtues of boldness and risk-taking through which one perpetually recreates and enhances one's identity. It is not embodied by a single narrative of gradual development, but by a number of discrete, even discrepant, achievements – brief lives as Nietzsche calls them.

Like the wired mode of life, entrepreneurship can be traced back to ancient times. Its roots lie in the civic humanist traditions of the Greeks and Romans, in which individuals promoted changes in their communities by directly engaging their fellow citizens through diverse organisations such as deliberative assemblies and productive associations. This tradition was continued in the early-modern period through the association-forming practices of merchants. What are the contemporary embodiments of these two forms of life?

The wired life

Wired productivity eschews the notion of a lifelong commitment. Such a commitment is seen as a way of being stuck, an impediment to personal growth, excitement and creativity. Instead of making a lifelong commitment to a profession, vocation or mode of working, wired people simply run with any of their several talents or inspirations. They may do this serially or all at once as portfolio workers. In this ideal, they may spend seven years of their adult lives as engineers, then go to business school and become consultants for another seven years, then buy into a winery and turn their full-time attention to that, and so forth. In the US, similar patterns are emerging among tradespeople. One might start out as a plumber's assistant, then join a company that offers training and a licence as an electrician. After climbing the ladder at work and accumulating some wealth, the tradesman might well take a six-month trip or buy a small ranch in Mexico, then go back to work as an electrician to support courses for a plumbing licence in order to start a small independent business. Of course, in the portfolio style, the affluent wired person might be a consultant and a vintner at the same time just as the tradesperson might work part-time as an electrician while starting a plumbing business.

It would be a mistake to view these lives as being made up of one mini-career after another. Rather, they are constituted by a series of projects. Such projects, in themselves, differ from careers in that they do not have the intended benefit of grounding the identity of an individual. Though they may include certain short-term commitments, they are not based on any commitment with oneself or others to live a particular kind of life. They are born out of an interest in expressing a talent or inspiration. So the good of a stabilising and identity-defining commitment is replaced by the priority of expressing and enhancing one's capacities. Whereas people who had careers joined vocational communities to which they were loyal and through which they could see the overall shape and style of their lives, people with projects are always trying out different project communities.

Members of these short-lived project communities can show intense passion, for example the software and hardware developers who work for many sleepless days and nights developing new products.[25] However, these groups feel comparatively little loyalty to either business or professional communities that require long-term commitments. Experiencing the passion involved in achieving a particular goal largely replaces loyalty to institutions or communities. In fact, project goals often clash directly with loyalty in order to achieve the desired 'breakthrough'. A project worker will commonly work with the company willing to support the project best, not remain with the one that originated the project or which has employed him or her for years.

Wired lives require recognition, but recognition that no longer carries the freight of a vocational identity. Since one passes regularly through different project communities, recognition within these groups involves recognition for having the wired lifestyle itself: following one's talents and inspirations, enjoying one's passions and recognising the free-and-easy lifestyle that grows from according oneself to such goods. Ongoing civic recognition, however, must therefore be neglected and does not play a large role in the wired life. One or another civic project might, of course, garner strong passions for a while. But wired people do not identify themselves with a community in which political action takes place. Generally, instead of valuing local communities, they explore various geographic areas in a nomadic style. While being on the move is a cost of the wired life imposed by the need (whether economic or psychological) for a new project, it is also one of its achievements.

Wired lives embody a radically new kind of personal autonomy. In the past, autonomous persons saw themselves as writing a coherent story of their lives each day. Wired lives, on the other hand, radicalise autonomy by freeing it from the weighty metaphor of authorship. In the traditional liberal conception of autonomy, each person has a duty to make the story of his or her life make sense, to make one moment build from the last, thereby contriving a continuous narrative of a life in its entirety. In contrast, living a wired life involves discontinuities in values, goals and commitments. Readily casting away previous modes of life and work makes the wired life remarkably able to respond to the concern of the moment whether it is a product, customer, health or spiritual concern. If it suddenly feels right to travel to India on a spiritual journey simply because one senses that one's spiritual interests have been neglected, then energies are turned in that direction. If a new marketing campaign feels right or is necessary because of competitive pressure, then energies are turned in that direction. This is, in effect, the life anticipated by Nietzsche, when he speculated that lifelong identities would give way to 'brief habits'.[26] The lives of wired people are more like collections of short stories than the narrative of a bourgeois novel.

While most do not have the resources to take time for a trip to India, following impulses is becoming widely accepted as desirable. Writers such as Geoff Mulgan see such actions as revealing the growing importance of valuing authenticity in the West. As he characterises them, they are actions driven by an attempt to have moral simplicity and purity.[27] While he is surely right, calling them attempts at pure self-expression registers a sea change in the meaning of the term authenticity. Today's authentic actions would have appeared as instances of inauthentic whim a generation ago. The poet William Wordsworth saw authenticity as leading a life focused on bringing out what made an individual's life (over its whole expanse) most meaningful.[28] In the wired form of life, spontaneity in responding to the current situation, rather than continuity of projects and relationships, becomes the test of personal authenticity.

In the new economy, such spontaneity has obvious commercial advantages. It is fast becoming a core competence for dealing with the changing needs of customers. As a consequence, the wired life has become more pervasive. Each day, high-tech and other high-performance businesses are organising more operations around projects. In the US, for example, it is estimated that as of 2000, 80 per cent of all Fortune 500 companies will have over half their employees on teams.[29] This signifies a remarkable change from the hierarchical organisations that blossomed earlier in the century. More importantly, however, it is not just the structure and organisation but the dispositions or mindset of its workers that will be altered. In response to this trend, the US Department of Labor has suggested that schools begin training students in such competencies as teamwork and project management.[30] Scientists, engineers, technicians and so forth increasingly see themselves as engaged in the project, not the company. With this kind of organisation, today's companies have learned to sustain even the 20 per cent average annual employee turnover experienced in their IT departments.[31]

As a matter of business practice, leading business thinkers like James Maxmin, former CEO of Laura Ashley, are developing new wired business models employing sophisticated logistics systems and non-hierarchical groups of creative employees who will run a pub or grocery delivery system until their inspiration flags. At that point, another group will take over.

Because it fits in so well with the fluid organisational structures coming into being, the wired life continues to grow. A recent Louis Harris poll shows that 22 per cent of American workers have wired values, and that 49 per cent can be characterised as migrating towards these values. Only the remaining 29 per cent of workers are still 'traditional'.[32] This study characterised wired workers as viewing loyalty in terms of contribution, job change as a vehicle for growth and advancement as based on performance. Traditional workers, in contrast, viewed loyalty as the reward for the promise of job tenure, job change as *damaging to career* and advancement as based on length of service. In contrast, wired workers reject job security as the driver of commitment to an organisation. These shifts in attitude are not surprising in the US economy, which has seen average job tenure for men, already the lowest in the industrialised world, fall 19 per cent between 1991 and 1996[33] after having already fallen over 10 per cent in the preceding decade.[34] These numbers could even underestimate the trend because of the aging workforce.[35]

While wired lives bring the spontaneous creativity that comes from openness and a highly focused albeit transient passion, they constitute a fairly radical break from the past in their shunning of dispositions and skills that depend on long-term commitments. Although sometimes a wired form of life is adopted during youth and develops into a more entrepreneurial form with age, nothing ensures that such a pattern will be followed. Indeed, it is hard to see why this should be. Following Maxmin's intuition that the business model best suited to the wired life is like that of rock groups that come together and dissolve when inspiration wanes, why should a wired worker learn to make the sacrifices it takes to keep an inspiration alive for the sake of communities of customers and workers when the inspiration is no longer fun? Because social goods such as stable identity, familial care, concern for a local community and broader adherence of civic and patriotic ideals demand being responsible to commitments that extend over large stretches of a lifetime, they can only have an attenuated role in the wired life. Nurturing them requires more than openness to the moment. They demand an acceptance of the dedication and sacrifice these obligations may entail. Since they are seen as roadblocks to personal development, such virtues are not honoured in the wired life.

The loss of such virtues is certainly not new. Cultural movements such as the Beats in the 1950s and many others in the 1960s called for shedding those communal ties that restricted indulgence in personal talents and predilections. Throughout earlier movements, however, such attitudes did not offer new ways of organising productive life. Indeed, they were often seen as alternatives to productive endeavour. Now, the accelerating trends affecting working life make it imperative to integrate the goods of personal spontaneity into productive life, in the name of flexibility.

Along with its creativity and flexibility, the wired life carries with it many moral hazards and political risks. At the personal level, there is the ever-present risk of failure. Of course, failure is a risk faced in all forms of life, but the risks incurred in the wired life have a peculiar severity. The wired life demands mobility for the freedom to move on from one project to another. When the wired person fails, he or she is thrown back into a social context or community that is perceived as confining rather than a source of sustenance. Since being on the move is one of the only aspects that ground the identity of the wired, loss of mobility not only signifies failure and confinement but also creates an acute crisis of identity.

Wired people who have become stuck in the dull, repetitive, unrewarding moments that occur during economic downturns will tend toward passionless disengagement, anomie and fatalism. Consider the emerging pattern that was developing in the US of discouraged wired workers simply moving back into their parents' homes during down times and awaiting some shift of fortune to move them out. There is little in wired life to protect those who lose their financial independence from becoming fatalistic and resentful, particularly because the wired lack the values of solidarity and self-sacrifice that such times might require.

The loss of identity and fatalism of the failed wired life are not only moral hazards. They are a political risk, as they endanger both the self-expressive aspirations and the careerist hopes of the working majority. When the economy turns down, there is not much difference between the concerns of wired lives and the concerns of more mainstream workers who cannot make ends meet. Both groups are likely to feel cheated. They may well turn against centre-left governments and parties to a right that promises opportunities they believe they have lost.

There is an uncomfortable precedent for this reaction in the coalition of disillusioned Essex men and women that helped to bring the Blair government to power. Many of these were people who during the Thatcher-Major years had been encouraged to adopt a form of life similar to wired lives. Rather than renting council houses, they were induced to take a risk and buy their homes – only to be mired in negative equity. Instead of pegging away in old-fashioned wage-labour, they were encouraged to follow their talents in setting up businesses – and then found themselves devastated by seesawing interest rates. The sense of being stuck in the tumult of unfettered free markets was one of the sources of Blair's landslide victory. The self-centred energies of the wired life turned against the political party that had promoted it. There is a risk of a similar shift of mood working against the Blair government when economic conditions become unfavourable.

Any economic setback that is serious and relatively long-lasting is likely also to evoke another perilous mood – nostalgia for the stability and security of the career. Nostalgia, after all, is actively cultivated among the wired, who already have a tendency to flirt with older practices like romantic love and elegant living. The practices are there to be tried on and let go whenever risk gets too high.[36] Why not nostalgia for the career? So long as the economy is in an upswing, those who had been left bereft of careers by downsizing and new technologies could hope to restart their working lives with another career. In times of economic adversity that hope is soon seen to be delusive. Now, regardless of the economic climate, that hope is slipping away ever further. Nostalgia about careers could evoke dangerous, reactionary politics.

The entrepreneurial life

Another form of working life is developing that could both rival the wired and give it the support it needs to flourish. Instead of being led by chance, talents and the inspiration of the day, the new entrepreneurial life is driven by bringing value to the community in which the entrepreneur dwells. For entrepreneurs, a meaningful life involves much more than the expression of personal capacities. It encompasses renewing the life of the community – through some new product or service, a political achievement such as a law or an institution, a cultural event or a new type of social service. Though some have tried to assimilate entrepreneurship with exploitative arbitrage, its creativity in the production of new institutions draws on the same creative energies and practices as those of political activists and cultural workers. The difference among entrepreneurs, political activists and cultural workers amounts to the different intuitions they have about social anomalies which inspire their innovations. Entrepreneurs see in social anomalies opportunities for new products and services; political activists see that some practice is being anomalously and unfairly discouraged; and cultural workers see an anomalous lack of understanding and appreciation of how people live.[37] Entrepreneurship can be practiced in many domains of life. What business entrepreneurs, political activists and culture workers all have in common is the initiation of a meaningful change, in a context of shared responsibilities and common history.

Entrepreneurs see themselves as dwelling in the history of particular communities and as actively enmeshed in social engagements. Of course, living in such historical communities is part of being human, but what matters is how that aspect of life is experienced and enhanced. Whereas wired people perceive this embeddedness in particular institutions and communities as a constraint on their personal creativity, entrepreneurs take it to be an essential good that grounds the very nature of their enterprise. It is precisely in the cultivation of commitments to their communities of customers, neighbours, employees and the like that entrepreneurs derive their success.

Self-realisation also has a different place in the life of entrepreneurs. The entrepreneurial worker or citizen does not explore his or her own talents and inspirations so much as his or her sensitivity to disharmonies, tensions or value conflicts that are shared by many in his or her community. The entrepreneur explores ways of living that lead to some way of resolving the disharmony, and gathers together a group of people to bring the resolution to full public effectiveness.

Entrepreneurs do not simply interpret and develop local knowledge, as the career holder does. They experiment with local knowledge in order to change it. As experimenters, they are neither abiding by the truths of earlier professionals nor following established routines. They are sensitive to how each day's situations are different from the previous day's. They are perpetually on the lookout for new ways to resolve abiding disharmonies.

Anita Roddick, for us an exemplary entrepreneur, was sensitive to the disharmony that had developed between caring for feminine dignity and caring for feminine attractiveness. As Roddick saw it, the cosmetics industry had reaped enormous successes by making women feel insecure about their attractiveness and sold cosmetics as a remedy for that insecurity. Instead of becoming resigned to the conflict between secure dignity and insecure attractiveness, as had other feminists who believed that the disharmony would only go away when patriarchy disappeared, Roddick committed herself to making a difference now. She realised she could sell cosmetics by drawing on such practices of pampering like taking bubble baths and getting manicures. She designed a sales space where cosmetics were placed alongside pampering toiletries and political pamphlets. Customers were urged to purchase only what made them feel good because of the pampering pleasure it produced and because it was also good for society. In this way cosmetics could cease to be tools of oppression and become tools for fun and reform at once.

Clearly, the Body Shop changed the rules of the game of selling cosmetics – numerous cosmetics companies have followed its lead. Yet its influence has not been limited to the sale of cosmetics. Because it can draw shoppers with little interest in toiletries and cosmetics, the Body Shop's claim to power has come from the attraction of shoppers to its distinctive atmosphere.

It appears that people like Anita Roddick are rare. How could enough of us lead entrepreneurial lives like hers? Feeling this way might well be a symptom of a dangerous resignation about the effects of globalisation. Of course, a similar question must have been asked in the early days of the career. Before the triumph of the guilds and merchants' associations, only clergymen, lawyers and physicians could have access to benefits we now associate with careers. Who would have believed that many could have them and the working majority could aspire to them? Still, we are not proposing that, even in commerce, we all become entrepreneurs as Anita Roddick did.

To replace careers with entrepreneurial activity does not mean that everyone has to go off and start a new industry-changing enterprise. First, we should remember that starting *any association* that brings a community something that people did not think possible counts as entrepreneurship. There are social entrepreneurs and civic entrepreneurs as well as commercial entrepreneurs.[38] Finding a way to establish and maintain a coffee shop in a town seemingly too small to support one surely counts as entrepreneurship as does founding a new social centre in the East End of London. Yet, we are not even suggesting that most people should be entrepreneurs in either the industry-changing, social, civic or the shopkeeping senses of the term. We suggest that *most* people will benefit by adopting the basic set of entrepreneurial practices in their working lives and applying them to the social institutions they have inherited from the past.

In the broadest sense, entrepreneurs produce value by sharing responsibility in developing new or ignored practices that could resolve some tension or relieve some disharmony present in their community or society. Hence, one does not have to leave one's company to become an entrepreneur. A simple case of an employee entrepreneur would be one who discovers Internet auctions, declares herself responsible for bringing their benefits to her company and gathers a small group of team members and allies together to bring this profitable change to the company. As more and more people in the company check with such an internal entrepreneur before making their purchases, she develops power, which she can leverage by making new offers inside her company.

The trends and forces that are doing away with the career open legions of possibilities for entrepreneurship. For example, one employee began to recognise that her company's outsourced graphics did not feel right. She began taking courses to develop a graphics skill and then offered to produce some of the designs with greater sensitivity to the company's concerns and brand associations. She would attend certain meetings that the outsourcing firm's employees were too busy to make. Jim Taylor and Watts Wacker point out the trend of company specialists negotiating deals for services or products that the home company could not, on its own, fulfil and then forming a new relation with the company to fulfil the agreement.[39] Similarly a professor we know has, with the help of some technical friends, started offering parts of his courses on the Internet for interested former students, parents and others he might entice to appreciate his discipline.[40]

In these examples, the employee exhibits the prime features of entrepreneurship: noticing that there is something not quite right, anomalous or in conflict. The employee then discovers a practice for resolving the anomaly – Internet auctions, graphics training and meeting attendance, a new service or Internet broadcasts – and makes an offer to provide services and products to resolve the practice, declaring responsibility for maintaining the offer. The employee gathers others who will help deliver the service and commits to alliances with others for mutual promotion, purchasing and so forth. As this happens more and more in the workplace, businesses will come to be increasingly constituted out of interlocking groups that see themselves as bringing a particular kind of commercial value to each other. In the US, Wells Fargo Bank is actively transforming each of its internal departments into businesses organised on such an entrepreneurial model. Just as one does not have to be a lawyer or a manager in a larger corporation to have a career, so one does not have to start a stand-alone commercial, social or cultural enterprise to be an entrepreneur. As Mulgan points out, our liberal sense of sovereign individualism blinds us to the way we act in a highly interconnected world. Seeing ourselves as only fully alive, aware and expressive within the associations that we start up or to which we belong can bring us an understanding that helps us cope with the way we are already beginning to live.

The constitutive elements of an entrepreneurial life, by contrast with the wired life, include many of the basic virtues of careers. The entrepreneur assumes a *defining commitment* to develop an ignored practice that will resolve a disharmony on a small or large scale. The entrepreneur *achieves recognition* by declaring himself or herself responsible for the resolution of the disharmony and by gathering people who have a similar interest. The entrepreneur values highly the *loyalty* of this core group and acts to preserve it. Entrepreneurs *support others involved in similar ventures*, as evidenced by the way successful entrepreneurs become venture capitalists. By supporting other entrepreneurial endeavors, entrepreneurs are actively building *new forms of community*. Finally, in their declaration of responsibility for a certain resolution of communal disharmony, they become *authors of a continuous life story*. Maintaining this continuity through difficult periods when inspiration fails is their responsibility, as it involves the successful resolution of disharmony and remaining loyal to the group that has been convened.

When entrepreneurs embrace these elements, an entrepreneurial world has many of the virtues of the career driven ways of life while also adding innovative change. Entrepreneurship is not the wired life. It is at the other end of a broad spectrum of new ways of working. There are also hybrid forms. The portfolio worker who promotes innovative medium-term projects as an entrepreneur and also joins on-going projects as a wired worker is one example. Another is that of lifestyle self-employment, in which individuals chose to remain largely independent from the organisations and project teams which use their services. These and other hybrids of entrepreneurship and the wired life may prove to be stable over long periods. But they are not free-standing. They depend on other practices and commitments they do not themselves require. Charles Handy, who has done as much as seems possible to make sense of the portfolio life, ends his book *The Age of Paradox* by calling each to find a larger purpose that makes it all worthwhile.[41] Entrepreneurship incorporates that larger purpose.

A new entrepreneurial world looks like a world of many interlocking small associations of people acting to resolve value conflicts. These associations may interlock inside a single corporation, local community or region, or across specific interest groups. The core difference between interlocking entrepreneurial associations and wired projects should be clear. Entrepreneurial associations will continue working to produce a successful resolution of the value conflict that aggrieves them as long as they can find any practical ground – usually some ignored practice or other – for moving forward. For a wired person, a project dries up as soon as the inspiration it expresses flags. The entrepreneur who takes responsibility for the resolution of the disharmony in a public declaration puts his or her identity on the line. That requires much more commitment than following an inspiration, energy or talent. In many cases, the entrepreneur's commitment will mean keeping the hope of his project alive among the many wired project groups she has working with her. To a wired person, the entrepreneur is clearly constrained by the expression of commitment. For the entrepreneur, in contrast, it is commitment that makes working life meaningful.

Conclusions

Given the two kinds of ideals the wired and entrepreneurial forms of behavior grow out of – Nietzsche's projects of an aristocratic caste and the civic humanist associations – it is no coincidence that the wired form of productivity fits well with global neo-liberalism's atomistic wealth creation and that entrepreneurship fits with a more socially integrated understanding of progress. Wired practices do not promote the nurturing of the kind of social 'we' for which people make sacrifices. Common goods such as the environment, law, education, health and the perpetuation of shared cultural achievements might flourish intermittently as one or another inspiration seems compelling. But promoting the shared goods of a common life depends on much more than the wired 'postmaterialist' concern with freedom, self-expression and quality of life.[42] It depends on mundane social goods that support actions when inspiration flags, such goods as depend on long-term cultivation of compromise, tolerance, trust and neighbourly warmth. Within the wired life, such common goods are experienced as personal goods that a group happens to share. Their role in sustaining a common life is rejected, or not understood.

The account of entrepreneurship we offer differs sharply from the current views of the neo-liberal right and the statist left. In those caricature views, entrepreneurship denotes a narrowly individualistic mode of life motivated exclusively by money. That account could never distinguish between a hedge fund operator who makes money cashing in on exaggerations in our expectations and an entrepreneur who develops a business that provides something new. Moreover, our account of entrepreneurship shows how the traditional common goods of communities can be promoted and enhanced in an entrepreneurial way of life. Crucially, it identifies what is most often missing from the politicised views: a concern for communities and for the well-being of others as a central motivation of successful entrepreneurship.

Of course, like the interpretation of wired life we have advanced, our account of entrepreneurship sketches an ideal type. As we have noted, there are many variations in practice. Nevertheless, we hold that our account is truer to common experience than the stereotypes of entrepreneurship cherished by the new right and the old left.

The wired life, which attracts greater numbers of people daily, draws us away from lives of continuity on which social solidarity has been founded. At the same time, for all the reasons we have set out, there is no way back to the world of work in which the career was central. We must look towards entrepreneurship as the form of working life that can renew the common values once supported by the institution of the career. With our financial and education institutions supporting the entrepreneurial form of productivity, wired lives may also thrive as a way of working in entrepreneurial associations. In a world that focuses its institutions on the support of entrepreneurial work, wired workers, whether they hold many projects serially or at once as portfolio workers do, may find themselves catching entrepreneurial commitment, and successful entrepreneurs might retire to wired forms of productivity. Similarly, practitioners of lifestyle self-employment may become successful entrepreneusrs.

However, these patterns will only emerge if policy promotes an entrepreneurial style of work. Policy focused only on wired or portfolio work will insufficiently nourish the culture needed for those workers to thrive. For many people, wired work will simply not offer a fulfilling alternative to careers. As a result, policies designed to be friendly to self-employment and portfolio work must be grounded in a larger framework that fosters entrepreneurship.

Policy in the wake of careers

Many of the inherited policies and institutions in Western societies have been shaped to fit the career as the central form of working life. Our school and university systems funnel young people into specific professions and occupations, encouraging investment in the expectation of lifelong careers. Our tax systems and banking procedures for granting credit are modeled on a world in which the credit-worthy majority are employees or professionals who will spend a working lifetime as practitioners of a single craft or vocation. Our pension systems reflect this same anachronistic pattern of working life. This inheritance is becoming an impediment to developing fully viable forms of working life. Radical reform is imperative.

Here, we can only sketch the outlines and guiding principles of such reforms. In two example areas – pensions and education – the goal is to make our social practices responsive to the new realities such that, in the aftermath of the career, working life can once again be meaningful for the majority.

Pensions and finance
The practice of a retirement with pension is far from immemorial. Toward the end of the nineteenth century, Bismarck successfully established the form of pension with which we are now familiar. It has been a device for saving well-suited to large paternalistic industrial and governmental bureaucracies and the careers they supported. Careers mirror the phases of the normal lifecycle. They demand increasing expertise along with natural developments of vigour and maturity and then come to an end when physical vitality begins to flag. The pension,

normally structured as an annuity, reflects the structure of a salary so that the career employee receives regular payments both while working and while retired. While working, the capital that the career produces or enhances is left to the company, union, pension fund or government. Part of that capital is the pension fund out of which payments (consisting mostly of returns on that capital) are withdrawn for the balance of the pensioner's life, again leaving the capital to the organisation administering the pension. In the nineteenth century, indeed until a decade or so ago, this relation to capital embodied in corporate structures and pension funds may have been a sensible way of organising the finances of the working majority.

The entrepreneurial life leaves much less room for paternalism and much more room for ventures and ownership of capital. Unlike career holders who see and seek a stable and consistent future, entrepreneurs are not content simply to put some money away with each paycheque. Entrepreneurs take the wealth they have generated with one enterprise and invest it in others. Many citizens will not want the security blanket of pensions to be simply torn away. But the paternalistic role now played by business, government and unions will have to change gradually into a role like that of investment regulators. 'Pension' money (or parts of it) might go through various transformations in the course of providing for an individual's future. It may serve as down payment on a house, capital needed in starting a new business, or as an investment in a new technology. It may even give support for projects involving community or family service.

This is not the place for detailed reform proposals – even if we were competent in the area. It is clear, however, that current arrangements for tax relief and annuity purchase were designed for an era when careers were the predominant form of working life. Traditional pensions are a hybrid of two quite different things – an investment plan and a retirement income. Except for the dwindling numbers who can expect pensions that are related to their final salaries, existing pension arrangements combine large restrictions on personal financial freedom with no assurance of a specific level of income in retirement. In particular, the requirement that 'pension money' be used to buy an annuity does not mesh with forms of working life in which retirement can be partial or temporary, and sometimes hard to distinguish from practices such as downshifting. To be sure, we need to discourage people from becoming a charge on the state, but that could be achieved by requiring the purchase of a small annuity sufficient for prevent poverty in old age. Otherwise, it would be more in keeping with entrepreneurial working life to merge the tax benefits that are presently given separately on pensions and investments, and give people freedom to do as they will with their savings.

We should keep a very open mind about the kinds of institutions that are best suited to providing the financial security and freedom that entrepreneurial workers need. Shareholder capitalism is not the only, nor by any means always the best, vehicle for meeting the financial needs of entrepreneurs. Pluralism in provision is essential. Inevitably, and desirably, the entrepreneurial life will be embodied in different institutions, depending on the type of capitalism, the history and the current needs of different economies. Entrepreneurial lives will be significantly different in China, Japan, Germany, Spain and Britain.

In the British case, it may be that mutual institutions can play a significant role in providing financial underpinning for more entrepreneurial forms of working life. As Charles Leadbeater and Ian Christie have noted,[43] mutuals are present in many sectors of economic life. In an entrepreneurial world, we would expect that they would become more diverse and more innovative in their practices than is commonly realised. As Leadbeater and Christie write:

'Mutuals can do more than survive; they can thrive in the twenty-first century service economy, because at their best they can harness two ingredients critical to success for modern enterprise – *trust* and *know-how*.'[44]

In particular, mutual institutions could be especially well-suited as vehicles enabling families and communities trapped in long-term poverty and lacking opportunity – the so-called underclass – to gain better control of their lives. As Leadbeater and Christie put it:

'Tackling deep-seated and multiple sources of disadvantage requires marshalling know-how from several different sources and professions in a joint effort, combining the tacit knowledge of people on the ground with the explicit skills of professionals. This is a central component in mutual approaches to community development'.[45]

This is only an example of a more general truth. The span of institutions we need, and that we already possess, is far wider than that recognised in the conventional discourse of left and right. We are not doomed to pick and mix only among the practices of shareholder capitalism, Rhinish capitalism and statist collectivism.

What is true for pensions is true for many financial practices. For example, financial risk analysis based on career status will increasingly fail to make sense. The same will be the case for qualifying people for financial products based on the cash flow that comes from careers. Financial products are already changing faster than banks and governments are able to respond to with sensible regulation. Governments and banks today are missing a sea of change that could easily drown their ability to address adequately a new world of financial products concerned with both equity and debt. The age of sophisticated products for all classes has arrived in the US, and is not far off in Britain.

As people become more entrepreneurial, they no longer see themselves primarily as consumers – whether of financial products or of other goods – but as *producers* of packages of financial products and as *designers* of the other goods in their lives. The financial institutions of the coming entrepreneurial era will help people produce wealth by creating both new products and new markets for trade. Internet auctions are one way we see new markets developing. Undoubtedly, just as large-scale entrepreneurs create and share wealth by selling shares in their enterprises, smaller entrepreneurs will want to do the same. Micro-credits extended to the very poor in Bangladesh by Muhammad Yunus's Grameen Bank are an example of the beginnings of these new financial institutions.

Education
The most fundamental changes, however, are needed in education. The role that schooling and university systems play in channeling young people into particular positions in the social division of labour has long been familiar to sociologists. In recent years, it has become an avowed

objective of government policies to engage in rational manpower planning. All such policies are doomed to be ineffectual. To turn schools and universities into narrowly focused vocational institutions is precisely the opposite of what is now most needed.

Many of the careers for which young people are trained in schools and universities will not survive throughout a working lifetime. It is self-evident that many activities require high levels of professional expertise. However, what young people most require from their schools and universities is not necessarily vocational training or training in traditional academic disciplines. Students now in traditional educational programmes, continuing education or retraining programmes need to learn the skills necessary for building value-creating associations.

The goal is *not* to transform everyone into industry-transforming business leaders. Nor are we demeaning the lives of those who will remain employees. Instead, we are proposing that the working majority will benefit from acquiring the skills and attitudes that go with the entrepreneurial life. The entrepreneurial life that we envisage requires training people to look for opportunities for value creation and to mobilise others to pursue the new value. In a world of entrepreneurial associations, both stand-alone and interlocking ones within larger enterprises, an education in value creation is suited for everyone. This reorientation of education aims at inserting a new core of entrepreneurial disciplines, some of which draw on older disciplines, and at leaving the other older disciplines around the new core.

As Tom Bentley has shown, there are a number of programmes in existence that assist people in adjusting to the new economy. These programmes emphasise much that fits with both wired and entrepreneurial lives: forming clearly-defined and understood objectives, access to a continuum of learning opportunities (in the classroom and in projects outside the classroom), real responsibility, collaboration outside the school peer groups, and identifying and celebrating concrete outcomes.[46] We go one step further. To make such projects more entrepreneurial, we would propose that those programmes that bring a new value to the community receive funding and other kinds of recognition above those that simply develop clear goals to express the talents of the learners. Likewise, we would give additional funding and credit to those programmes that involve declaring oneself responsible for some activity around which one assembles others. Training people in disciplinary and practical skills with a strong project orientation is not enough to produce an entrepreneurial economy with a wide dispersion of entrepreneurial skills.

We are concerned not so much with the institutions in which education currently occurs – though it is self-evident that most of it takes place outside schools and universities – nor with particular educational methods, but with the assumptions that animate education itself. Whether or not they had merit in the past, our traditional educational practices are failing to equip people for the world in which they will have to live.

Our current educational, vocational and corporate cultures orient people to become takers of requests who solve problems. They presuppose a world in which givers and takers of requests fall into neat categories, and problems come to us already defined. It is useful to help students understand that the problems of businesses are not only, or even mainly, problems of cash-flow, accounting or marketing. They are problems of human relations within the business and with those whom it serves. Encouraging students to take a wider view of the problems they face in their working lives is an essential part of developing their problem-solving abilities. But by itself it does not promote entrepreneurial awareness, or success in the new world of work.

We recognise that better problem-solving abilities may well be useful for a short time after people leave school. The new engineer, the new journalist, even the new manager takes the requests of those above him, turns them into a problem to be solved elegantly and solves it. But some years later – unless the request taker is unusually flexible and talented – a global business will hire a newly trained request taker who knows all the new problem-solving technologies and will let the older one go. What does the request taker do? Does he or she look for some new organisation to make requests of him or her? In the new economy, this search is as likely to fail as the education that led to it has failed.

Today, to work effectively, people need to be able to make *offers* to produce special value for customers, whether these customers are consumers or other groups within the same organisation. Problem solvers do not think in these terms. They expect the world to reveal itself in a series of discrete problems. But as life becomes more mixed, more cosmopolitan, more focused on niche concerns and more technologi-cal, there are fewer disciplines or businesses that can go along with a set of clear problems. In this world, people need to make offers to poten-tial employers, to the market or to their communities. Developing such offers is the first step towards creating enterprises, and learning how to develop offers is the first priority of education.

We must therefore educate people to see themselves in terms of their socially valuable skills, intuitions, emotional sets and abilities. At present, we teach people to solve the problems presented to them in ways that are personally rewarding. In an economy animated by entre-preneurship, such education will lead at worst to failed careers and at best to ever faster wired lives.

For people to learn to make offers, however, they will have to learn how to listen to their fellows differently. And to teach them to build enterprises that deliver those offers, they will need to abandon the current *quid pro quo* form of network building and learn instead how to build and coordinate commitments, manage power, build and main-tain trust, and establish compelling identities. In short, people will need to learn some basic skills that we have assumed, up to now, belong to leaders alone.

Education for entrepreneurship involves changes in four domains. First, people will have to learn to listen to the concerns of their fellows and identify them with certain historical narratives. We can no longer teach people to see themselves as outside of, above, or at the end of historical communities. Training people to regard themselves as free from their history and community imbues them with a false sense of autonomy. We live inside traditions. We need to see ourselves as carri-ers of definite historical narratives.

Research at Business Design Associates suggests that entrepreneurs generally understand themselves as developing and enhancing one particular historical narrative as opposed to others. We have always known that political leaders do this, and their success has often turned on their ability to articulate these narratives. Again, we see this as a necessary supplement to the set of capacities Tom Bentley says need cultivation for the new economy. In our highly plural societies, it is not enough for people to improve their understanding of their place in any one narrative. They have to be able to connect it with the narratives of others. Helping people to place themselves within more than one historical community is as decisive for entrepreneurial intelligence as the developing their reflective and cognitive capabilities.[47]

Having this capacity means listening to people as they are, with all their contradictions and fragmentation. Currently, we are taught to see people as coherent persons with stable identities and not as the increasingly complex mixtures of diverse traditions, roles and competing practices they are. Worse, we learn that people are largely in control of their ways of seeing the world and choose their values. So we listen to people as if they were rational choosers, and fail to hear what they are saying as creative subjects.

Second, entrepreneurial listening requires listening to people to identify the conception of the good life that motivates what others say and do. Entrepreneurs must hear how people's conceptions of the good life are in disharmony. Anita Roddick did this in listening to how women lived for dignity and beauty. Steve Jobs heard how people wanted both high-tech convenience and freedom from mainframes. Akio Morita, Ted Turner and the rest of today's entrepreneurs all achieved entrepreneurial success by listening for seemingly irresolvable conflicts.

Third, we need to teach people the disciplines of managing commitments and developing and maintaining trust. People are schooled to think of themselves as performing actions such as developing a presentation or fulfilling a function such as sales. Although many entrepreneurs talk about their actions in these ways, they do not simply act as though they were engaged in activities or fulfilling functions. Entrepreneurs build their enterprises by developing networks of agreements or commitments from others. They are not solving determinate problems or adhering to a fixed business plan, but using their skills to negotiate relationships with others so as to make their enterprises work better. Jim Clark, founder of Netscape and two other multi-billion dollar enterprises, makes this point over and over again. As an entrepreneur and conceptual artist, he sees his ability to build strong teams as the most important aspect of his success.[48] Crucial among these skills is the ability to inspire trust. At present, the skills involved in striking up, maintaining and reviving trust remain in the hands of a small cadre of professional negotiators, diplomats and managers.

One of the objectives of an entrepreneurially-oriented education would be to make these skills accessible to the majority of people. We should encourage people to think of themselves and one another in non-standard ways. Today, for instance, we are trained to speak in a way that delivers other people either facts, the more standard the better, or solutions to problems. Some of the new emphasis on dialogue (as opposed to debate or discussion) risks standardising speech inasmuch as it is about exploring common ground and sharing in what is common.[49]

In contrast, entrepreneurial intelligence requires finding where people are conflicted. To live entrepreneurially, we should train people to see the benefit of, imagine and negotiate non-standard agreements with each other – especially when they share conflicts and come out on opposite sides. Like dialogical thinking, this involves inculcating in people the skills they need in order to ask what the problem – whether in an office, a school or a business – *means* to the people who present it, or suffer from it. But understanding meaning includes examining the structures of power in which the problems arise, and by which they are partly constituted.

Fourthly, therefore, people who engage in entrepreneurial life need to be trained to read the world to see how and where power is maintained. Power in political and commercial life is poorly understood as a force and studied under the heading of barrier creation, which means promoting circumstances that make a competitor's way of doing business uneconomical. But power is much better understood under the arts of continually building new, material connections to values a majority of people in a community care about while positioning competitors as having material connections to values the majority despises.

Bill Gates of Microsoft, for instance, exercises power by integrating competitors' ideas into his operating system in order to give his customers a seamless business solution. If he were simply trying to undercut the pricing of his competitors' products—which is how he has been positioned by his competitors—he would raise even more worries about property rights than he has. Indeed, until he integrated the Microsoft Explorer Internet browser to undermine Netscape, he had successfully positioned his competitors as producing disruptions in computer use. Anita Roddick exercises power in the same way as Gates by producing entertaining retail experiences and positioning competitors as boring or selfish.

Entrepreneurs need to learn value-based strategies for forming alliances to destabilise, dislodge and reconstitute power. Such training would draw on certain parts of the disciplines of strategy, marketing and the interpretive arts of the humanities. Educational practices that leave people with a view of the world as composed of discrete problems, and of themselves as problem solvers or request takers, have little future in a world that is being continuously transformed by new technologies and new global relationships.

Educating people to become active shapers of their lives involves inculcating the art of constructing an identity for oneself. Likewise, in building enterprises, entrepreneurs learn to project the virtues they have institutionalised in their organisations. Today we confuse producing an admirable identity with image management. Because of this confusion, we split the skills for projecting an identity among a number of different disciplines including journalism, spin-doctoring, strategy, advertising, expository writing, literary criticism, psychology and ethics. In reality, knowing and describing ourselves is the hard work to which the liberal education has now and then – always at its best moments – been dedicated.

Turning self-knowledge into a strategy for the creation of value has remained a skill in the hands of entrepreneurial leaders. In the age of the Internet, where the beginning of work will be in constructing one's web page, building personal and corporate identities may well become the most necessary and valuable skill anyone, entrepreneur or not, could have.

Any account of the kind of skills needed by the new world of work would be incomplete if it left out the emotions and moods that animate, or undermine, entrepreneurial behavior. Daniel Kahneman and Amos Tversky have shown that people routinely react differently to the same risks, depending on how much their perception of them enables them to see the potential loss. In short, non-entrepreneurial people tend to be overly risk averse.[50] The implication of Kahneman and Tversky's studies seems to be that most people are simply not cut out for the entrepreneurial, gain-focused life that new technologies are making possible. Francis Fukuyama made much the same suggestion in his book, *The End of History and the Last Man*, where he argued that the end of affluence may be a condition of boredom not unlike that which Nietzsche ascribed to the diminished 'last men'.

These studies appear to support the common belief that the entrepreneurial life is suited only to a heroic few. In the work of Business Design Associates, however, we have found that moods of anomie and resentment drive the focus on loss that plays a large role in the results of such studies. Many high-level managers and specialists, even many who seem to have adjusted to the wired, project-oriented life, live on the edge of a mood of anomie. Many whose faith in careers has been wounded find themselves filled with a silent resentment directed against company executives, political leaders, stockholders, the rich, the poor, educators and sometimes their own parents. They focus on a past that can never be honored enough because, as Nietzsche observed, it has always been lost. In contrast, entrepreneurs and entrepreneurial employees express quite different moods. Where some talk about the danger of getting carried away, entrepreneurial types talk about coming windows of opportunity that they feel approaching. Where others are possessed by resentment, these entrepreneurs are possessed by wonder.

By themselves, changes in mood and perception are rarely enough to change lives. Many other things are needed. But clinging to ways of organising work that, like the wired life or the declining institution of the career, fail to meet vital human needs breeds moods that guarantee failure. Insofar as our current educational practices tacitly support these flawed models of work they are schooling young people in disappointment. And entrepreneurial training today must start with that disappointment. Tom Bentley has argued rightly that education needs to focus on cultivating dispositions and that we must take Daniel Goleman's work on emotional intelligence seriously.[51] But we need to go beyond training children to identify, evaluate and shape their dispositions. We should help them capture the sense of meaning that goes with entrepreneurial success.

With most educational programmes still preparing our children for a world of careers that is in decline, the wired life seems to many to be the wave of the future. We believe that, though it will surely be a strand in the new working practices that are emerging, the wired life will thrive only if it is supported by the more community-oriented life of entrepreneurship. Despite all the wired life's virtues of spontaneity and the peculiar kind of personal autonomy it makes possible for those who live it, it will never give fulfillment to the working majority. It leads all too easily to anomie and mere casualisation. Likewise, mourning the old world of work that new technologies are making redundant offers nothing to the generation that must find its way today.

The new technologies that are changing our working lives so deeply will not, by themselves, give meaning to the new world they are creating. If work is to be meaningful for most people in the near future, we need to rethink some of our inherited institutions and practices and stand apart from the fashions of the present. We need to think of our working lives and those of our children not in the anachronistic framework of careers or the narrow self-realisation of the wired life, but as opportunities for commitment, innovation, and entrepreneurship.

Notes

1. 'New US Workers: Flexible, Disposable; 'Temping of America' Rolls On,' *Boston Globe*, 3 April 1994.
2. Sennett R, 1998, *The Corrosion of Character*, WW Norton, New York, pp18-31 & pp136-148.
3. GPO, 1999, *Statistical Abstract of the United States*, GPO, Washington DC.
4. Leadbeater C, 1999, *Living on Thin Air*, Viking, London, p192.
5. Birch D, Haggerty A and Parsons W, 1997, *Who's Creating Jobs?*, Cognetics, Inc, p7.
6. Data from US Small Business Bureau quoted in 'Hired Guns Boom in Workplace', *Los Angeles Times*, 2 February 1993; and in Cohany SR, 1996, 'Workers in Alternative Employment Arrangements,' *Monthly Labor Review*, October 1996, pp31-45.
7. 'The Growth of Self-Employment,' *Worklife Report*, vol 10, no 4, pp8-10.
8. Stevens J, 1995, 'Flexible Working Has Yet to Kill the Traditional Job,' *People Management*, vol 1, no 23, p57.
9. Leadbeater, 1999 (note 4), p192.
10. Bryson J, Keeble D and Wood P, 1992, 'The Rise and Role of Small Service Firms in the United Kingdom,' *International Small Business Journal*, vol 11, no 1, pp11-22.
11. 'Full-time Workers; Endangered Species,' *The Arizona Republic*, 24 May 1995.
12. Fierman J, 1994, 'The Contingency Work Force,' *Fortune*, vol 129, no 2, pp30-36.
13. A Conference Board Survey quoted in Bellinger B, 1995, 'Temp Hires on Rise,' *Electronic Engineering Times*, 2 October, p103.

14. Gutner Block T, 1995, 'Brains for Rent,' *Forbes*, vol 156, no 3, pp99-100.
15. Fierman, 1994 (note 12), p33.
16. Dennis WJ, 1996, 'Self-Employment,' *Journal of Labor Research*, vol 17, no 4, pp645-661.
17. Segal LM, 1996, 'Flexible Employment: Composition and Trends', *Journal of Labor Research*, vol 17, no 4, pp525-541.
18. Contingent workers are broadly defined as part-time, temporary, or out-sourced by National Association of Part-time and Temporary Employees. NAPTE estimate quoted in the 1996 article 'Temporary Staffing Still Growing, but a Little Slower,' *Managing Office Technology*, vol 41, no 9, p34. Other estimates, with more restricted definitions of 'contingent', are as low as 25 per cent (see Fierman, 1994, p30).
19. Boyle E, 1994, 'The Rise of the Reluctant Entrepreneur,' *International Small Business Journal*, vol 12, no 2, pp63-69.
20. Stevens J, 1995 (note 8), p57.
21. Coyle D, 1999, *The Weightless World*, MIT Press, Cambridge, Massachusetts, p103.
22. 'Paying for Performance: A Survey of Merit Pay,' *Industrial Relations Review & Report*, no 569, ppSS4-SS7.
23. The distinction between globalisation as an inexorable historical process powered by new technologies and globalisation as a particular political project is made Gray J, 1998, *False Dawn: The delusions of global capitalism*, Granta Books, London.
24. See Bryan L, 1999, *Race for the*

World, Harvard Business School Press, Boston, Massachusetts, pp39-66, for an account of the different rates of development of global markets and of the new economy.

25. Kidder T, 1981, *The Soul of a New Machine*, (1997 edition), Modern Library , New York.

26. Nietzsche F, *The Gay Science*, (1974 edition), Vintage, New York, p295, pp236-237.

27. Mulgan G, 1997, *Connexity*, Chatto & Windus, London.

28. See Trilling L, 1972, *Sincerity and Authenticity*, Harvard University Press, Cambridge, Massachusetts, esp pp92-94.

29. Johnson C, 1999, 'Teams at Work,' *HR Magazine*, vol 44, no 5, pp30-36.

30. US Dept of Labor, 1991, *What Work Requires of Schools: A SCANS Report for America 2000*, US Dept of Labour, Washington, DC.

31. Cone E, 1998, 'Managing that Churning Sensation', *Information Week*, 4 May, p50.

32. '1999 Emerging Workforce Study,' [website]. This survey might have captured the views of entrepreneurial workers as well as wired workers.

33. Blumfield M, Gordon J, Picard M and Stamps D, 1997, 'The New Job Mobility', *Training* vol 34, no 5, pp12-14.

34. Princeton study by Henry Farber quoted in Samuelson RJ, 1996, 'Are Workers Disposable?' *Newsweek*, vol 127, no 7, p47.

35. GPO, 1999, *Economic Report of the President*, USGPO, Washington DC, and 'The End of Jobs for Life?' *Economist* vol 346, no 8056, p76, UK, p104.

36. See Coupland D, 1992, *Generation X*, St Martin's Press, New York.

37. Spinosa C, Flores F and Dreyfus HL, 1997, *Disclosing New Worlds*, MIT Press, Cambridge, Massachusetts.

38. See Leadbeater C, 1997, *The Rise of the Social Entrepreneur*, Demos, London, and Leadbeater C and Goss S, 1998, *Civic Entrepreneurship*, Demos, London, for examples of civic and social entrepreneurship.

39. Taylor J and Wacker W, 1997, *The 500-Year Delta*, HarperCollins, Ne York.

40. See Professor Hubert L Dreyfus's 'online' course at http://socrates.berkeley.edu/~hdreyfus/198/.

41. Handy C, 1995, *The Age of Paradox*, Harvard Business School Press, Boston, Massachusetts, pp173-192 & pp249-280.

42. Abramson PR and Inglehart R, 1995, *Value Change in Global Perspective*, University of Michigan Press, Ann Arbor, pp9-24.

43. Leadbeater C and Christie I, 1999, *To Our Mutual Advantage*, Demos, London.

44. Leadbeater and Christie, 1999,p8.

45. Leadbeater and Christie, 1999, p21; for a broad examination of mutuality as a principle of social organisation. See also Mulgan, 1997 (note 27).

46. Bentley T, 1998, *Learning Beyond the Classroom*, Routledge, London, pp42-53.

47. Bentley, 1998, 136-138.

48. Lewis M, 1999, *The New New Thing: A Silicon Valley story*, WW Norton, New York.

49. See, for instance, Yankelovich D, 1999, *The Magic of Dialogue*, Simon and Schuster, New York.

50. Kahneman D and Tversky A, 1979, 'Prospect Theory: An Analysis of Decision Under Risk,' *Econometrica*, vol 47, no 2, pp263-291.

51. Bentley, 1998 (note 46), pp133-134.